THE BIG SKY BOYS

And Life on the Spinnin' Spur

Todd Linder

EQUUS
FILM & ARTS FEST
2020
WINNIE WINNER

AUTHOR SHOUT
RECOMMENDED READ
2019
READER READY
AWARD

READERS' FAVORITE
FIVE STARS

Monday Creek Publishing LLC
mondaycreekpublishing.com

1. Big Sky Boys, The   2. Juvenile Fiction - Western   3. Juvenile Fiction – Ranch Life

ISBN: 978-0-578-51100-9

To Lauren, Trey, Jordyn, Rylee, and Mackenzie,
who have put up with Bopa telling fanciful
stories at bedtime.

Contents

The Big Sky Boys and the Surprise Chicken

Out in the West, where there used to be more cows than people, there were ranches both big and small. One of those ranches was the Spinnin' Spur Ranch. It was kind of a small spread with a cook called Cookie, three ranch hands, a few broken-down nags, a cow dog, some chickens, and, of course, cows. Now, in those parts you didn't ask a new hand where he came from or much about his past. Most of the time the name he gave you was just a nickname like Peewee, Montana or Rooster. Now, if you thought Peewee was a small cowboy, you'd be wrong. He was a mighty tall and sturdy young cowboy. Montana was a tall, lean drink o' water, and Rooster was about as big as a banty rooster.

Cookie could whip up the meanest grub a cowboy ever ate. Every mornin' the boys sat down to a breakfast of beefsteak, eggs, grits, and pancakes. Sometimes the boys would have a pancake-eatin' contest to see who could hold the most flap-jacks. And when they did, they could barely make it to the corral to saddle up for the day's work. When they mounted up, those old nags could almost be heard to be groanin'. The boys worked the hard life of a cowboy, mendin' fences, makin' hay, fixin' windmills, and such, as well as punchin' cows. So, when they were done workin' and dinner was over, most nights they fell into bed fast asleep with their boots on.

When the boys did have a little spare time on their hands, livin' in the middle of nowhere, they made their own kind of mischief. So, it was one mornin' with daylight to burn, Rooster got the bright idea to see if he could rope a chicken runnin' around in the ranch yard. Round and round he ran, a-swingin' that rope and chasin' chickens and roosters this way and that. The boys were hootin' and hollerin' encouragement and directions to Rooster and addin' to the general carryin' on. "Go left!" "Go right!" "Throw the loop now!" "Don't let her outrun you, son!"

Rooster's pet armadillo named Albert, who normally slept in a box on the bunkhouse porch, was so spooked with all the carryin' on that he scuttled under the bunkhouse and wouldn't come out for at least an hour after things settled down. Well, sir, with all the dust and commotion and chicken-squawkin', old Cookie knew somethin' was goin' on at the Spinnin' Spur that he wouldn't approve of. He stormed out of the ranch house ready to do battle with a big spoon in one hand and a fryin' pan in the other. He marched up to the boys and hollered, "What in this world are you doin' to my chickens?"

Rooster, his rope tangled around his feet, piped up and said, "We was just havin' some fun, Cookie. We wasn't hurtin' nothin', honest!"

"Well, how about this, you knot heads! If'n you scare up them chickens and run the meat off 'em, all you gonna get to eat with your dumplin's is chicklets 'stead of chicken! And if them chickens ain't layin', you got no cake, no cookies, no pies, and no pancakes!!"

Peewee stared at Rooster, who stared at Montana, who stared at Peewee as if to say, "We never thought of that!" The boys looked down and shuffled their boots in the dust, all red-faced, and mumbled, "Sorry, Cookie, won't happen no more."

As Cookie walked back to his kitchen, a plan began to tickle his brain. He sat down and wrote a letter to the Quincy Exotic Bird Emporium in Kansas City, and then mailed it the next time he was in town.

One mornin' two weeks later, the boys were walkin' to the

ranch house with high hopes of a breakfast feast. What they found was an empty kitchen and nothin' at all smellin' like pancakes or anything else for that matter. On the table was a note from Cookie that said he was in town and wouldn't be back 'til dinnertime and that they were on their own. "All I kin find is these here cornflakes!" Peewee wailed as the boys pondered on the long day ahead. The boys walked down to the corral with some grumblin' bellies, but I can tell you, those horses breathed a sigh of relief when the boys mounted up!

When Cookie did finally get back later while the boys were on the range, he scooted into the house all mysterious-like with a box under his arm. Next mornin' just at the crack of daylight, he snuck into the ranch yard and opened the box so a strange bird could make its exit. Then he ran screamin' into the bunk-house, yellin', "Now look what you done to my chickens! You scared 'em so bad they laid a monster! It's a chicken that ain't no chicken!"

The boys stumbled out of their bunks and onto the porch in their long john underwear, boots, and hats, except Peewee who accidentally wore his bunny slippers. They stared at the most peculiar sight they had ever laid eyes on! There in the middle of the ranch yard were some chickens runnin' away from a bird not even close to lookin' like a chicken! It had all kinds of different-colored feathers stickin' up from its head and the biggest tail feathers they had ever seen. When that bird commenced to squawkin', it was the most awful noise they'd ever heard! For the next few weeks, at odd hours of the day and night, those awful noises startled the daylights outta the boys. Fact is, he pretty much out-roostered the rooster in the mornin'. Rooster said, "We ort to shoot the thing!" but Peewee replied, "You might ort to be thinkin' about no pancakes!" Rooster quick-like changed his mind. The boys weren't gettin' much sleep, and when they asked Cookie if the squawkin' was botherin' him, he just yelled, "What?" and pointed to the cotton in his ears. They thought about herdin' the critter out onto the prairie where maybe a coyote might just happen to find it but figured Cookie would know what happened, and that wouldn't be a good thing at all.

One evenin' in the bunkhouse while Rooster and Montana were playin' Old Maid and Peewee, bein' the one with the book learnin', was readin' through the letter P in the dictionary by the light of the kerosene lantern, Peewee let out a thunderous *"By cracky!!"* He hopped off his bunk and smacked the book on the table where the boys were playin' Old Maid and pointed to the very bird struttin' in the ranch yard. "That's no odd kind of chicken!" he said, "That there's a no-foolin', genuine peacock!" Well, the boys gave each other a flabbergasted look and started laughin' so hard they fell off their chairs.

"Well, I'll be," said Rooster, "We been spoofed!" Montana and the rest of the boys came up with a plan and next mornin' the boys had a talk with Cookie. Peewee, bein' the spokesman, said, "That strange bird is gettin' mighty big and plump-like. Maybe we ort to have him for this evenin's dinner." The look on Cookie's face when he saw the huge knife in Peewee's hand and Rooster pointin' to the picture in the dictionary said it all. He finally admitted to the prank he'd played on the boys. They all had a big ol' laughin' spell there in Cookie's kitchen, and he said he'd make them the best dinner they'd had in a while at the Spinnin' Spur, just minus the "chicken."

Cookie agreed to find the bird a good home, and pretty quick things were back to normal and peaceful-like at the Spinnin' Spur. I can tell you, everybody was mighty happy not to have that awful ruckus to wake up to. The boys went back to eatin' like cowboy kings and decided to take up playin' horseshoes instead of chasin' chickens. They thought it best to save the ropin' for the calves and heifers.

The Big Sky Boys Go To Town

Now, the Spinnin' Spur Ranch was a busy place most days, weeks, and months. What with chores and ridin' the range, Peewee, Montana, and Rooster didn't get too much in the way of entertainment or fun. So, when they got the chance to go to town with Cookie, they usually took it. After their usual belly-bustin' breakfast of piles of flapjacks, eggs, grits, and spuds, not to mention enough coffee to float a rowboat, the boys commenced to get gussied up. They took turns gettin' a bath in the old washtub and flipped a nickel to see who got the first go-round in the clean water. Then, it was get on your go-to-town jeans and shirt, slick back your hair if you had some - Cookie's was gettin' a mite sparse - with Dr. Jack's all-purpose hair tonic, and wrap it all up by shinin' your best boots.

Now, you might expect that, bein' cowboys, they'd ride

their cow ponies to town, but you'd be wrong. The ranch had a not-so-new pickup truck the boys affectionately called Gus. Gus could be a mite ornery when it came to startin' and had been known to start with a good swift boot to the right front tire. Nobody could figure out why it worked, but it did. Once you got old Gus movin', he'd move right along. The question was, for how long. Sometimes it'd take two or three sharp kicks twixt the ranch and town. Now, the ritual every time the boys was about to mount up old Gus and head for Horned Toad was to flip a nickel to see who'd ride shotgun in the cab with Cookie. With four fellers goin', it meant that two of 'em had to ride in the bed of the pickup. That meant that by the time they got to town, two of the boys could be pretty windblown and covered with dust from head to foot. "Let me see that nickel!" said Rooster, squintin' at both sides to see if there was some trickery goin' on. Not findin' anything suspicious, Rooster figured if he got a couple of large paper feed sacks and cut eyeholes and a hole for their mouths, they'd keep from lookin like they'd ridden fifty miles in a dust storm. It was a mighty peculiar sight to see two paper sacks ridin' in the back of old Gus when they rode in to town. They got more than a few odd looks from folks on the boardwalk outside the general store.

Well, sir, one of the first things the boys did in town was

to head for the barber shop for a store-bought haircut since they hadn't seen a haircut for a good spell and figured they didn't want to look like they was wearin' a horse's mane. Old Pete the barber, havin' seen the boys ridin' in to town covered with a feed sack and wantin' to have some fun, asked, "Where you boys been? You smell like horse feed er molasses." Peewee and Rooster grinned and didn't take no offense. After gettin' a clip, they walked the main street takin' in the sights, gettin' some ice cream, and pickin' up the mail at the post office. When they got to the other end of town, they arrived at the general store. Now, Rooster had got wind of Cookie's birthday comin' up next month, and he and the boys decided they'd throw a real humdinger of a cowboy birthday bash at the ranch and maybe invite a few neighbors and friends of Cookie's from town. The trick was to get Cookie out of the way so they could do some birthday shoppin'. They had already planned for Montana to take Cookie across the street to the café, where they'd get a cup of coffee and some of Miss Vera's raspberry pie Cookie was so fond of. Miss Vera and Cookie could share recipes and chat.

While Rooster got started at the general store, Peewee headed out on a hunt for that special present he thought Cookie'd be tickled with. He strolled over to the Horned Toad

Lawn 'n' Pawn to see what he could find. A little while later, he proudly carried out a long package wrapped up in cardboard and put it in the bed of old Gus. Rooster came out with party supplies all wrapped up secret-like along with the stuff from Cookie's list. When Rooster asked Peewee what was in the package, he just grinned and said, "Never you mind, son. I don't want anybody spoilin' the surprise."

They headed over to the café for an early supper before headin' for the Spinnin' Spur. By the time they was ready to head home, it was gettin' on to sunset. After the nickel flip to see who got to ride shotgun, Montana, who lost, says, "I ain't wearin' no tom-fool feed sack!" and got out his duster coat and hopped in the back. Rooster, who had no coat with him, stuck on the feed sack and jumped in. The ride back to the Spinnin' Spur was uneventful, and Gus had no complaints. When they got back late in the evenin', they unloaded the supplies. Peewee almost got caught by Cookie with his long cardboard package but managed to get it into the bunkhouse on the sly. The boys went to bed soon after puttin' up old Gus to be ready for the next long spell of ranchin' but vowed they'd have Cookie's party all planned and ready to roll the next month.

The Big Sky Boys Throw a Birthday Bash

Every year at the Spinnin' Spur there were birthdays. Some of the boys weren't so sure of the exact day, so Cookie thought it'd be best if they just all celebrated on the same day so nobody'd feel left out or embarrassed. Thing was, though, Cookie could be downright crotchety and ornery, especially if his cake flopped in the oven. The boys were kind of fond of him, or at least of his flapjacks. Because of that, they thought it'd be wise to make a big deal out of his birthday. They figured they'd send invites to a few of Cookie's town friends and spread the word to some of the neighborin' ranches up and down the road. High on the town list was Miss Vera from Horned Toad's best and only café, who Cookie was kind of sweet on. The biggest thing was keepin' this shindig top secret. Now, since ranchin' is no picnic, most ranch folks are always lookin' to rest a mite. Those invited was mighty happy to be honorin' one of their own and said they'd be ready.

The boys started plannin' this bash by figurin' what games to play. The games weren't for the faint of heart, but then we're talkin about cowboy country. So, the list was set: wild cow milkin', cowboy croquet, blindman's bull tail grabbin', sunflower seed spittin', and, to wind it up, a piñata bash. With that chore done, they had to figure out this piñata thing. Montana, bein' the quiet type, said, "How 'bout a peacock piñata? After that chicken spoof Cookie pulled, it'd be kinda fittin', don't ya think?" Rooster and Peewee snuck into the ranch house and rustled up all the old copies of the *Horned Toad Gazette* they could find and scuttled back to the bunkhouse. "I forgot the flour and glue," whispered Peewee, and ran back and grabbed them. Over the next couple of weeks, the bunkhouse looked like a tornado in a newspaper office. Strips of newspaper were strung everywhere. Every night the boys were cuttin' strips of newspaper and mixin' flour, water, and glue to make the piñata. By the time they were done, the piñata looked more like a wounded dinosaur than a peacock. Rooster found some left-over barn paint, and the boys got it real colorful.

On the day of the party, the rest of the plan began to take shape. Miss Vera called to ask Cookie to cover the café for her 'til noon. Cookie of course said, "Miss Vera, I'll be there quick as a jackrabbit." The boys had to put up with cornflakes for breakfast that day, but there was no complainin'. As soon as Cookie showed up at the café, Miss Vera picked up ice for makin' homemade ice cream and the cake ingredients and headed for the ranch. So, while Cookie was jawin' with half the town at the café, Miss Vera was busy makin' the cake and one of the boys was churnin' a bunch of homemade ice cream. With the help of some of the neighbors, all the games were set up and ready by the time Cookie was on his way back to the ranch. When Cookie rolled up the ranch road in old Gus, the company'd come and hid. As soon as Cookie stepped out of Gus, everybody popped out of where they were hidin' and yelled, "*Happy birthday*!!"

Well, Cookie just stood there with his mouth hangin' open like a Venus flytrap and commenced to grinnin' a big ol' grin. Rooster yelled, "Let them cowboy games begin!" Everybody went to their first game. The games went well 'til some poor soul actually connected with that tail at the bull tail grabbin' and gave 'er a good yank. The bull went plumb wild chasin' guests all over the ranch yard. The general feelin' after that was it would be a mite safer to stick with the sunflower seed spittin' contest or the piñata bashin'.

13

After all the flour, glue, and newspaper the boys had used on the piñata, folks came nowhere near to breakin' it! Rooster grabbed a shotgun from the bunkhouse and yelled, "Stand back folks. I'll get 'er opened up!" The piñata blew into shreds, and candy and newspaper flew everywhere. After an hour or so, it was time to eat. Along with the cake and ice cream, the boys had made a plumb delicious barbecue. By that time, the fun was windin' down, and the boys decided it was time for the presents. After the town folks had delivered theirs to Cookie, Peewee came proudly carryin' the long package he'd gotten from the Lawn 'n' Pawn in town and handed it to Cookie. When the wrapping came off, there in Cookie's hands was a sorta beat-up but pretty good trombone. Everybody stared and wondered what had gotten into the boys to give such a present to Cookie. But he looked as pleased as punch! He said, "I always wanted to learn some kinda musical instrument, and out here it won't matter how much I toot!" When he said that, Montana looked sideways at Peewee and whispered, "You sure this was a good idea, pardner?"

As it was gettin' on towards sundown and chore time, everybody helped with the cleanup and the party broke up. The boys were pretty beat and made it an early night. The next mornin', the boys were awakened by the most unearthly noise they had ever heard. It was worse than a peacock! When they ran to the bunkhouse porch in their nightshirts and boots to see what was goin' on, there was old Cookie standin' on the back porch of the ranch house in his faded red long johns, his cheeks puffed way out blowin' on that trombone for all he was worth. "I thought I'd get in some early practice and be the alarm clock all at the same time!" hollered Cookie. The boys looked at one another, and Montana asked Peewee the very question that Rooster was about to ask. He said, "You sure they didn't have no harmonicas?"

Makin' Music at the Spinnin' Spur

Well, sir, it was bound to happen. Cookie's trombone playin' was becoming a problem! First off, he was scarin' the chickens in the mornin' blastin' his trombone. In fact, the poor rooster quit crowin', which meant that with their ears stuffed full of cotton the boys were gettin' up late almost every mornin'. The next thing you know, the hens quit layin', but the thing that topped it off was Percy the bull deciding that all that tootin' was a challenge and chasin' Cookie off the porch and into the ranch house! "I'm thinkin' I better trade this here noise-maker in for somethin' a mite quieter," said Cookie that night at supper. "Maybe we ought to start our own music-makin' with ya!" replied Rooster excitedly. The next time they were in town, they all wandered over to the Horned Toad Lawn 'n' Pawn to trade in Cookie's trombone and see what they could find. Cookie traded his beat-up but pretty good trombone for a concertina. Rooster found an old, sort of used-up bass drum with the words Horned Toad High on it. Peewee spied a kazoo, and Montana came up with a pretty good kind of used-up guitar with only a little crack that he thought tape might fix.

They started practicin' on the bunkhouse porch each evenin' after supper. At first, all that racket disturbed Albert, Rooster's pet armadillo, so much that Rooster had to crawl under the bunkhouse porch and encourage him to come out. Rooster thought he'd better come up with a way to keep Albert from getting all excited. After playin' around with some wire, yarn, and milkweed fluff, he created some kind of earmuffs, which took time for Albert to get used to.

The boys practiced for several months and even came up with their own musical creations. Peewee wrote a song called "Blue Moon on the Prairie." Rooster came up with his own, which he called "The Armadillo Waltz in honor of Albert." Montana suggested that being cowboys and all they could not get by without practicin' "Home on the Range."

One day, Rooster rode his cow pony to the mailbox and gathered the mail. His face broke into a big ol' grin when he showed the flyer that came in the mail to the boys that evenin' at practice. "There's goin' to be a talent show in town next week! I think we ort to enter!" The boys looked hard at Rooster to see if he was serious. When they saw that he was, they looked at one another and shrugged. "Why not?" said Peewee. "I think it'd be fun!" "Well, I ain't sure I want to be up in front of a crowd," replied Montana, who was always kind of shy. "I say let's do it!" Cookie said with a grin to match Rooster's. The boys sent in their entry and practiced all the harder.

When the big night came, the boys showed up at Horned Toad High dressed in matching shirts, jeans, and hats. They had entered as the Big Sky Bunkhouse Orchestra. There was Charlie Chuggle doin' rope tricks to music and Penelope Pringle recitin' poetry. The Loyal Order of Hoot Owls in their feathered costumes had a kazoo band. They performed a number while doing what they called the Hoot Owl Stomp. The stomp was interrupted, however, when Willard Whistle the fire breather was practicin' his fire breathing and accidently set one of the Hoot Owl costumes on fire. By the time the local fire department had put it out, the poor Hoot Owls were completely soaked and their costumes were ruined. Last to perform were the boys from the Spinnin' Spur. They started with their original musical numbers and finished up with "Home on the Range," which brought tears to the eyes of every rancher and cowboy in the place. The audience broke into wild applause, and the judges awarded the Bunkhouse Orchestra first prize. Miss Vera from the Horned Toad Café was thrilled and invited the boys for coffee and pie. With the moon shinin' bright on Old Gus the ranch pickup, the boys headed home to place the trophy, which was a brass horned toad, on the fireplace mantle and get ready for another day of ranchin' on the Spinnin' Spur.

The Big Sky Boys and the Double Trouble

Now the boys at the Spinnin' Spur thought things would get back to normal after Cookie's big birthday bash. Boy, were they wrong! Cookie got an important phone call from his sister askin' if her eight-year-old twins could come for a visit out West. The boys were of a mind it might be fun to show 'em what a working ranch was really like. They borrowed a couple a ponies from a neighbor and brought in a wild cow from the range so the boys could have some milk.

When the day came for the twins to arrive, Rooster lost the nickel flip, so he was elected to fire up old Gus and head for the bus stop in Horned Toad. When the bus arrived, the driver and passengers got off shakin' their heads in exasperation and mumblin' somethin about wild billy goats. Last to get off were two red-headed twins, and when Rooster saw the grins on their faces, he knew right off the boys at the ranch were in for it! They were both wearing a pair of cap pistols in holsters, and their pockets were bulging with caps. This most certainly had Rooster nervous right from the get-go!

After throwin' the twins' suitcases in the back of old Gus, Rooster and the twins headed for the Horned Toad General Store to pick up some things for Cookie and get the twins some cowboy duds. Rooster went to the grocery side to pick up a few things for Cookie. By the time Rooster headed back to the dry goods side, the twins had created an awful commotion! The manager whispered real fierce-like to Rooster, "Please, don't ever bring them boys in here again!"

The ride back to the ranch wasn't much better. The twins kept up a terrible chatter askin' all kinds of questions 'til Rooster pulled old Gus over and asked, "You young'uns ever rode in the back of a pickup truck?" They thought that would be great fun. Once in the back, they started shootin' their cap pistols and carryin' on 'til one of 'em almost fell out. That finally settled them down for the rest of the ride to the ranch.

Back at the ranch, Cookie introduced the twins to Montana and Peewee. Rooster, lookin' about as exasperated as the bus driver, gave the boys a raised eyebrow and said real quiet-like "Boys, we're in fer it!" While Cookie went back to his kitchen to get supper, the twins began to chase around the ranch yard exploring. Before the boys could yell *"Don't!!,"* the twins had jumped from the hayloft onto a pile of hay under the hayloft, barely makin' it and scatterin' chickens from here to yonder! While Montana was milkin' the half-wild range cow, Brett or was it Brad began to grab old Bossy's tail and started pumpin' it for all he was worth. The cow, not takin' kindly to that nonsense, kicked over the milk and about stomped old Montana. Montana, so mad he could a spit nails, asked, "What do ya think yer doin?!!" Brett or was it Brad said real innocent-like, "Everybody knows that's how you get milk from a cow!" Montana sent them to see if they could help Cookie with supper and tried to get at least a few ounces of milk from Bossy. That evenin' after supper, the boys were lookin' real mournful-like at each other in the bunkhouse 'til finally Peewee said, "Two weeks!!"

For the next few days or so, it was nothin' but one prank after another The final straw was the night they got back from a long day of punchin' cows on the range to find Rooster's pet armadillo Albert painted about four different colors, and when they finally put their heads on their pillows, they heard startled frogs croakin' in their ears!

The boys began layin' plans to teach the twins a lesson.

The next mornin' while the boys were still asleep, Montana, real sneaky-like, went to the ranch house and got the twins' cowboy hats. He turned 'em upside down and began to puttin' boot polish on the sweatband inside the hats. When the twins took off their hats at lunchtime, everybody got a good laugh except the twins. Next mornin' when the twins got dressed and put on their boots, they found them full of shavin' cream. Now, the twins realized they were getting some of their own back, but it wasn't over yet. The boys had borrowed a couple of billy goats and a couple of sheep. Rooster told 'em, "All cowboys learn steer wrestlin' by wrestlin' billy goats." By the time the goats were done, they had butted the twins all over the corral. The next day, when the twins showed up to ride the sheep in the mutton-bustin' "practice," they were wearin' some mighty wicked-lookin' pointy spurs and big grins. "You young'uns ain't puttin' spurs on them sheep! Fact is, we gotta sorta tie ya down on them sheep so ya don't get throwed." said Peewee. The boys had borrowed the biggest sheep they could find and fixed a kinda riggin' so the twins could be tied down real secure for the ride. As soon as the twins were mounted, each on a sheep, Montana might have just forgotten to close the corral gate, and Rooster might have just set off a string of about fifty firecrackers. The sheep lit outta the corral like they were on fire with a wolf chasin' 'em and headed down the road toward home five miles away. The boys hung on the corral fence laughin' 'til they could hardly hold on. Finally, the sheep with the twins screamin' for all they were worth were about a speck on the horizon. The boys looked at each other, and Montana said real slow-like, "Well, I spose we gotta go get 'em." "Do we have to?" Pewee sighed. The boys mounted up on their cow ponies and rode hard to catch up. When they finally caught up, they roped the sheep and ended the fun. The twins' eyes were about big as could be, and they were totally outta breath. Rooster said, "You young'uns learnt your lesson?" All the twins could do was nod. The rest of their stay, the twins were as good as gold. Several days after the twins had left; Cookie got a letter from his sister askin' if the twins could come back next summer and maybe stay the whole summer. She also added that the doctor told her she was havin' another set of twins. The boy's jaws dropped in disbelief when they heard that news. They walked back to the bunkhouse shakin' their heads and mumblin' somethin' about quittin'.

Rooster Rides the Line

"Let me see that nickel!" grumbled Rooster.

Montana handed him one and said, "Sure, pardner." Montana gave Peewee a quick wink as he did it. Every chore the boys had to do seemed to start with a nickel flip to see who got to do it. Since Rooster always seemed to lose, he began to think that Montana and Peewee had got ahold of a trick nickel.

Rooster said, "Next time, we'll use my nickel!"

Now, in the old West there was a time when there weren't any fences, and cattle and cowboys roamed free. After a while, though, the whole idea of having your own spread all fenced in took hold, and that meant lots more work. There were miles of fence that had to be checked and cows to be looked after. This time, it was Rooster's turn to ride the line fence. The other boys helped him fix up a pack with tools, grub, fence wire, and what-ever else they thought he'd need. So, one frosty mornin', Rooster saddled his old nag Sassafras, loaded up his pack horse Goose Bump, and got ready to ride.

"So long, pardner, don't take no wooden nickels," said Montana with a wicked grin.

Peewee piped up and said, "Son, make sure yer fence is horse-high, pig-tight, and bull-strong!"

Rooster decided it'd be a good idea to take along Curly, the old cow dog. Rooster and company rode for miles through rough country, seein' nothin' but coyotes, buzzards, and prairie dogs. After quite a few miles, they came to what cowboys call a line shack. She wasn't much to look at, just a little cabin to make some grub in, get some shut-eye, and keep warm. After unloadin' some supplies to stock up the shack and puttin' hob-bles on old Sassafras and the pack horse to keep 'em from wan-derin' off, Rooster and Curly settled in for the evenin', hopin' to get some supper and shut-eye. Now, you'd think that a dog that could chase and corner an ornery range cow or bull would be sorta brave, but old Curly was kind of a scaredy-cat. Before Rooster could get in his first winks, a hoot owl started hootin,' and first thing you know that dog was scrabblin' to crawl under the blanket with him. Rooster pushed the animal outta the bed and yelled, "Git over there and lay down by the wood stove, you old flea-bag!" Curly just crawled under the bed.

Next thing you know, there was a growlin' outside and old Sassafras and the pack horse were goin' crazy. "Mountain lion!" yelled Rooster and called for Curly. Curly, however, liked it just fine under the bed and wasn't comin' out. Well, sir, Rooster in his long johns grabbed his shotgun and headed out the door, stepped on a cactus, and shot wild, just makin' some noise. After gettin' the cayuses settled, he limped back into the shack. "You good-fer-nothin' bag of bones!" he yelled at Curly. Things calmed down, but the rest of the night, every once in a while in his sleep he grumbled, "Worthless cow dog!"

In the mornin', after some beans, bacon, biscuits, and coffee, Rooster saddled up Sassafras and the pack horse and started ridin' the line. After fixin' some fence and catchin' a few cows to doctor, they took time for some trail grub of cold biscuits, coffee, and left-over bacon. This went on for several days and lots of miles. Then, one afternoon while the horses were hobbled and Rooster was fixin' fence, Curly spotted a rattlesnake and began dodgin' this way and that barkin' up a storm. Sassafras and the pack horse were gettin' a mite excited, so when Curly backed up too close, old Sassafras sent him sailin' ten feet in the air, rollin' over and over and landin' with his backside on a cactus. Rooster had to spend the next hour pullin' cactus spines from Curly's backside. "You crazy dog!" yelled Rooster. "You'll play with a rattler but won't protect me from a lion!"

That night, at the last line shack before headin' back to the ranch house, Rooster and Curly had just gotten settled down for the evenin' when all of a sudden Curly got to barkin' and settin' up an awful commotion.

"What you thinkin', Curly, is it a kitten er a rabbit yer all bothered about?" Rooster said sarcastically.

When Curly wouldn't settle down, Rooster finally let the dog out in case it was somethin' more serious. As soon as Curly bolted out the door, Rooster was as sorry as he could be! There, just outside the shack, was a good-sized polecat! As soon as Curly got near the thing, it let loose with a smell that would uncurl a pig's tail! When Curly tried to high-tail it back into the shack, Rooster shut the door fast as he could. "You can jest stay out there all night, you crazy dog!" he yelled. After a spell, Curly crawled under the line shack, and that awful smell wafted up through the floor and kept Rooster awake most of the night.

Next mornin', that smell was still mighty strong, and Rooster tried wearin' a bandana doused with horse liniment on his face, which didn't help much. Curly followed at a distance from Rooster and the horses with his tail tucked betwixt his legs. After a while, Curly gave a mighty yelp when he stepped on a big cactus, and Rooster finally felt a little sorry for the dog. With a big sigh, he said, "Come on up here, you." He hauled Curly up in front of him on the saddle, and they headed for the ranch house.

Now, by the time they were on the home stretch and the ranch house was in sight, they both stunk mighty bad. The rest of the boys and Cookie met up in the ranch yard, sniffin' the air and lookin' at each other. "You smellin' what I'm smellin'?" said Peewee. They all looked in the direction of the smell, and puttin' two and two together pointed at the sight of Rooster and company headin' up the ranch road.

"*Hold up right there*!!" they all yelled. They walked down the road and spoke to Rooster from a distance.

"We got skunked!" Rooster yelled back.

"You ain't comin' no closer 'til we get you both sorted out!" yelled Cookie. "I'll go get the wash tub and all the tomato juice we got. You can start to strippin' down, and the boys will get you some clean duds. You ain't comin' no closer 'til you smell better!"

Well, the boys got Rooster some clean duds and set up a

washtub and filled it half full of tomato juice, horse liniment, hair tonic, and whatever else they could find. They dug a deep hole and buried Rooster's stinky clothes. They also set up a pup tent so Rooster could stay away from the bunk house 'til the stink went away.

Rooster asked, "Could you all bring Albert to stay with me?"

When they brought him, Albert sniffed the air and made a beeline for the bunkhouse as fast as an armadillo can go. When Rooster was finally allowed back in the bunkhouse, he was mighty tickled to be back in his own bunk, and said, "I ain't ever takin' that fool dog anywhere again, and next time a chore comes up, *we will use my nickel*!"

Peewee Gets the Art Bug

Peewee gave Montana a totally flustered look as he stared at himself in the bunkhouse mirror.

"What's that thing on your head?" asked Montana.

"Nothin', just a little somethin' I found," replied Peewee.

That little nothin' was a French-lookin' beret he'd secretly ordered from a catalogue. Peewee had been bitten by the art bug! Peewee had always been a doodler. He would draw on whatever he could get his hands on. He would draw on post-cards, used envelopes, or letter-writin' paper. Now, don't mis-understand, Peewee was no artist. His creations didn't usually look anything like what he said they were. His dogs looked like frogs, and his horses looked like giraffes.

"Kind of a strange-lookin' nothin'," commented Montana.

"Well, if you must know, it's my French paintin' hat!"

"I reckon if we wear cowboy hats fer herdin' cows, you can wear a paintin' hat fer paintin'." said Montana. "You plannin' to slap a coat of paint on the inside er the outside of the bunkhouse?" he said with a sly grin.

"I'm gonna paint real pictures!" said Peewee in a huff. "I might even get famous!"

The next day, Peewee looked around the Spinnin' Spur 'til he found some left-over barn paint. Then, he went to ranches up and down the road 'til he had collected everything from barn paint to tractor paint. He mixed in his "secret" ingredient to make them into different colors and then was almost ready to start. He washed up a bunch of feed and flour sacks and hung them out to dry. These would be his canvases. Until his store-bought brushes came in the mail, he settled for chicken feathers that he trimmed to the right size with a scissors.

Then he sat. He sat and sat and sat some more.

"Whatya waitin' for?" asked Rooster one evenin' as he sat down next to Peewee, who was wearin' his French paintin' hat.

"Waitin' for inspiration," Peewee said, sounding discouraged. "All us artists has to get inspired before we can paint."

"Well, why not just paint what ya know?" suggested Rooster. "You know about cowboyin' and horses and ranchin'."

Peewee pondered that for a while and decided that maybe Rooster was right. He began paintin' up a storm. He covered every wall in the bunkhouse with his "masterpieces." While all this paintin' was goin' on, poor Albert was getting' spotted head to tail with every color Peewee had used. As Rooster and Montana looked at these works of art, they turned their heads one way and then another trying to figure out what they were. The horses reminded Rooster of giraffes. The one that was supposed to be Rooster's pet armadillo Albert looked more like a turtle with an armadillo tail. Peewee painted what was supposed to be Rooster standin' beside his giant prize pumpkin Oscar and what he said was a portrait of the rest of the boys. What Rooster and Montana saw looked like a stick figure layin' underneath a monster pumpkin and three stick figures sittin' on giraffe-lookin' horses.

"Well, they're mighty interestin'," said Cookie, trying to be polite.

Finally, the day came that Peewee had been waiting for. There was an announcement in the *Horned Toad Gazette* about a local art show, invitin' all local artists to enter. When the boys asked Peewee what he was going to paint, he just grinned and said, "You'll have to wait and see."

After several days of ponderin' what to paint, Peewee came up with an idea for his art show masterpiece. Since he had no photograph of his idea, he decided he'd have to paint it from memory. He set up his paints and flour sack canvases. Then, he grabbed his chicken-feather brush, closed his eyes, and painted. When he thought it was done, he opened his eyes and grinned. His grin faded as he squinted and turned his head first one way and then another.

"Well, now, that don't look at all like my memory!"

After his braggin' to Montana about becoming famous, he was quite embarrassed. He hid his painting, and when the boys asked about it, he just shrugged. Cookie found it hidden in a closet in the ranch house and decided he'd enter it in the art show for Peewee. The day of the art show came. Everybody except Peewee was all gussied up and ready to head to town.

"Ain't goin'," said Peewee.

There was no way they were going to persuade him to go, so the others mounted up old Gus the ranch pick-up and headed for Horned Toad. After secretly entering the painting, Cookie and the boys looked at all the other paintings. At the end of the day, they were shocked when a rich fella from the East bought Peewee's masterpiece, which he said was the nicest-lookin' eggplant he'd ever seen.

"It was supposed to be a mama grizzly bear!" Peewee said with a hoot when Cookie handed him the money. "Reckon I better paint more pictures with my eyes closed!"

Montana, Rooster, and Cookie looked at one another, shrugged, and began to think about takin' up paintin' with squirt guns!

The Big Sky Boys and the Bronc Bustin'

Well, sir, anybody that knows a thing about cow punchers in the old days knows that they needed their horses. Now, back in the day before all them newfangled ways of ranchin', the horse was the only means of gettin' from here to yonder. Cowboyin's hard on horses, so ranches had to keep a string of them constantly bein' broke for ranch work, and that's not just hard work but downright dangerous! Why, those mustangs could throw a feller ten feet outta the saddle into the corral dust, and I don't mean no soft landin' neither! More than one cowboy had his bones broke and his brain jostled a time or two.

So, it was the same thing goin' on at the Spinnin' Spur. Every month, the boys, Peewee, Montana, and Rooster, took turns bustin' some of the meanest, orneriest nags this side of yonder. They'd tie up a bronc to a post in the middle of that big old round pen and with one of 'em ridin' pick-up horse, the second would be throwin' a saddle on the bronc of the month and the third feller would commence to mount up before that ornery cayuse could lay down in the dust or try rubbin' the saddle off on the post. When it looked like the rider was half ready, the second hand would let go of the rope and let 'er rip!

This month, it was Rooster's turn to be the one gettin' rocketed out of the saddle leather and landin' spread-eagle on the ground. Now, Rooster'd been at this business since he was knee high to a hay bale, so he'd seen a thing or two. Today, though, Rooster had a secret weapon to keep from gettin' *kerwhumped* when he landed in the dust. See, just down the road a piece on the next spread was none other than "Sam the Slam," whose real name was Samuel Kerwinkle, a Horned Toad High star football lineman. Well, sir, Rooster took a ride over to the Flyin' K ranch on the sly and came back with a pretty good-sized gunny sack tied to his saddle horn. "What ya got in that sack?" asked Montana. "None of your beeswax!" answered Rooster, sounding suspicious-like. The boys looked high and low to find it, but Rooster had hid it deep in the hay in the barn. They finally gave up but made several guesses, at which Rooster just smiled like a cat lickin' cream.

So, when it was Rooster's turn to mount up on that ornery

horse, he walked out of the barn all geared up. The boys were aghast at first. Then they busted out laughin' so hard that when Peewee fell on the ground, he let go the rope and they had to lasso that horse all over again and get him retied to the post. Montana, never bein' one to show much feelin', sat sideways on his pick-up horse with one leg slung over the saddle horn. He let out a slow whistle and a sly grin as if to say, "Can't wait to see this." Now, what they was so tickled about was when Rooster came out of the barn, he was wearin' a complete football uniform with shoulder pads, helmet, and britches topped off by chaps, boots, and spurs. He glared at the boys and yelled, "What's so all-fired funny?" "Ever' thing'!" squalled Peewee. "Son, you are definitely in the wrong place er the wrong business!" "I'm tired of gettin' my bones busted up," Rooster replied.

Montana, real quiet-like, said, "You sure that ole nag's gonna let you get ten feet from him?"

"Well, I spose we could blindfold the critter," Peewee piped up.

So that's what they done. But when the boys gave that bronc his head and he heard them shoulder pads a-flappin' and looked back at that strange-lookin' rider, he jumped higher, twisted farther, and reared back steeper than any bronc ought to.

He took one final jump, and Rooster rocketed out of that saddle like a cannon shot! He shot over the fence between two fence posts like he was makin' a touchdown at a football game. He lay there in the dust for a while 'til Peewee ran and got a bucket of water from the horse trough and doused him.

When he came to, Rooster asked, real groggy-like, "Did I bust him?"

Peewee told him, "Son, you didn't even make it ten seconds in the saddle! It weren't one of your brightest ideas. I'm thinkin' you ort to give back that football outfit and go back to cowboyin' the old-fashioned way."

Rooster admitted he probably wouldn't try that again. That night, the boys stuck Rooster in a hot bath in the washtub and rubbed him down with horse liniment so he could get to sleep. It was a few days before he could sit a saddle, and he had to tie a pillow on it in order to ride. From then on, Rooster vowed he'd stick to the tried and true cowboy ways for good.

About the Author

As an elementary educator in years past, Todd spent many hours reading aloud to students in hopes of not just entertaining them but also of instilling in them the love of being lost in a book. As a boy riding horses, Todd often wondered if he had been born a hundred years too late and what it would have been like to cowboy with the likes of C. M. Russell in Montana or with the hands on the King Ranch in Texas. He's realized at least part of that dream by living in Montana, "the last best place."

About the Artist

Logan Rogers is a fine artist and illustrator who has been drawing and painting ever since he could hold a crayon. In school, he was one of those kids who drew whenever the teacher wasn't looking. His illustrations, geared toward children's literature, showcase expressive characters and settings, and tell compelling stories. He lives and works in southern Ohio, with his family and many pets.

www.ingramcontent.com/pod-product-compliance
Lightning Source LLC
Chambersburg PA
CBHW031940090426
42811CB00002B/244